Nathaniel Paine

Remarks of the Early American Paper Currency of Massachusetts

Nathaniel Paine

Remarks of the Early American Paper Currency of Massachusetts

ISBN/EAN: 9783743346765

Manufactured in Europe, USA, Canada, Australia, Japa

Cover: Foto ©ninafisch / pixelio.de

Manufactured and distributed by brebook publishing software (www.brebook.com)

Nathaniel Paine

Remarks of the Early American Paper Currency of Massachusetts

REMARKS

ON THE

EARLY PAPER CURRENCY

OF

MASSACHUSETTS.

Read before the American Antiquarian Society, April 25, 1866,

BY NATHANIEL PAINE.

CAMBRIDGE:
PRESS OF JOHN WILSON AND SONS.
1866.

Fifty Copies on Large Paper.

No. 23.

Worcester Nov 10/[?]

C H Hart
    Sir

I have sent in a package to Mr J A McAllister the copy of my "Remarks" you ask for in your letter of 5th inst.
You can call there for it and pay him the $2.50.

I will endeavor before long to send you some of the Antiquarian Society Reports which were wanting in your set.

Resp'y Yours
Nath. Paine

EARLY PAPER CURRENCY.

It has occurred to the writer, that a somewhat extended report, even though it be crude and imperfect, upon the small collection of early paper-money of Massachusetts now in possession of the Antiquarian Society, and, in connection with that, upon the history of Massachusetts paper-currency, might not be uninteresting to the members of this Society. The paper-money of to-day is the cause of much legislation, of wide-spread controversies, of numerous dissertations upon the safety and probable value of government paper-currency; as, a hundred and fifty years ago, there were similar discussions and examinations of the system of an issue of paper-money.

The difficulty found in tracing the history of the early paper-currency suggests to us the advisableness of this Society gathering into its collections all that would assist the future antiquary in the study of the financial history of our times.

In order to understand fully the influences which led our forefathers finally to resort to the expedient of paper-money, we must know how they practically understood the term " currency ; " and a short review upon currency in general may not be out of place.

Currency is defined by Webster as " that which is in circulation, or is given and taken as having value, or as representing property." This definition, in its broadest sense, admits of a great variety in the articles which may be used in trade or barter as a valuable consideration. At the present day, however, currency or money is almost universally confined to the metals, gold and silver, or something which is based upon them; although we now have, in this country, a currency which is not directly based upon those metals, but more upon the confidence we have in the strength and stability of the government, and the immense productive interests of the country, as displayed in the industry of our people.

Gold and silver have for many ages been recognized, by the general consent of the business world, as the standards of value. They constitute the money of all commercial nations, and are considered as the standards by which we measure the value of all other articles.

The earliest recorded mention of a metallic currency is in the account of a purchase and sale of land, in the twenty-third chapter of Genesis. Abraham bought a piece of land of Ephron, that he might bury his wife therein, the price of which was four hundred shekels of silver. "And Abraham hearkened unto Ephron; and Abraham weighed to Ephron the silver, which was named in the audience of the sons of Heth, four hundred shekels of silver, current money with the merchant." This was not coined money, like the Jewish or Israelitish shekel of later days, but lumps or pieces of silver, cut into different sizes, to weigh a certain quantity, as shekels, talents, or drachms.*

The Jews also used for money certain articles of jewelry, which were called jewel-money. This consisted of personal ornaments of specified weight, which were used in payments. The jewels mentioned as given by Abraham's servant to Rebekah are examples. "The man took a golden ear-ring of half a shekel in weight, and two bracelets for her hands, of ten shekels, weighed gold."

The precise date of the invention or origin of coined money, like many other useful inventions of man, is lost in obscurity; and it has been ascribed to different ages and countries. Herodotus ascribes the first issue of gold coin to the Lydians; the first silver coins are said to have been coined in the eighth century by the Greeks of the island of Ægina; others ascribe to the Asiatics the first issue of coined

---

* The coined shekel, a fac-simile of which is in the cabinet of the Antiquarian Society, has, on its obverse, the sacred cup of manna, and on the reverse the rod of Aaron.

money. The strongest testimony would seem to give the Greeks the honor of the invention. The Jews are said to have practised the art about the year 144, B.C., long after the use of positive coins in other countries.

Various are the materials which were used as currency, by different nations, in past ages. The Carthaginians had money somewhat of the nature of bank bills, but made of leather: this material was also used as currency by Frederic II. at the siege of Milan; and by John of France while paying for his ransom to Edward III. In the thirteenth century, money was found in use, in some parts of Asia, made of the middle bark of the mulberry-tree, cut in round pieces, and stamped with some mark or design. The penalty of counterfeiting this money was death.

The Gauls used for money gold and iron rings of a certain weight. This kind of currency was also in use among the Egyptians, as seen in their sculpture and painting, where figures are shown weighing it out, and others writing down the amounts. This money passed by weight, and not by count. Ring-money was also used in England and Scotland till it was superseded by the coinage of the Roman Empire. The Roman coin circulated in Britain till about A.D. 414. The Saxons, succeeding the Romans in England, introduced their own coins; and, during the reign of Baldred, which ended A.D. 823, the first silver penny was coined in England.

The aborigines of this country also originated and used coins of various substances. Our knowledge of their money is gained from the exhumations of the mounds of the Mississippi Valley, in which have been found shell, jasper, agate, pearl, mica, native gold, silver, and copper, made into the shape or form of money, mostly rude, but many showing signs of great skill. Money, apparently made from human bones and the bones of animals, has also been found in the mounds. The shell-money, found in the tumuli, is made principally from the shells of the genus Unio, and from small, spiral, fresh-water shells. It is a question which may well be enlarged upon and investigated by some of our associates interested in the history of the mounds of the South-west, whether these specimens alluded to were really used as a circulating medium, or as ornaments among the earlier Indian tribes. That they were so used by the later tribes, we know from the history of the colonists. Shell-money or wampum, also called bead-money, was for many years used as currency among the colonists of New England and the Indians; and, as late as 1704, it is said to have been circulated in Massachusetts for small change. Wampum was made by the Indians from oyster and clam-shells, also from the shell of the periwinkle: holes were bored in small pieces of the shell, and strung upon sinews as we string beads. The dark beads, less than an inch in length, and bored longitudinally, were of the highest value, and highly esteemed by the Indians, more so than the English gold or silver.*

William Wood, in his volume entitled " New England's Prospect," first published in 1634 (a reprint of which has lately been issued by the Prince Society), says, in speaking of the Narranganset Indians: "Thefe men are the moft curious minters of their Wampompeage and Mowhakes, which they forme out of the inmoft wreaths of Periwinkle-fhells. The Northerne, Eafterne, and Wefterne Indians fetch all their Coyne from thefe Southerne Mint-Mafters." From the inferior tools used by the Indians in its manufacture, the currency was quite rude. In the New York Colony, however, the Dutch residents made some improvement in the appearance of the strings of beads. They used white and blue beads, made from the muscle or sea-conch, and displayed more taste in the arrangement. A string one fathom long was called worth four guilders, or about one dollar and sixty-six cents of our currency.

Mr. Hickcox, in his late publication on the paper-currency of New York, says that "Wampum was introduced into New England by Isaac De Razier, in 1627, and passed at the rate of five shillings per fathom." And Bronson, in his account of Connecticut currency, says that "the different colonial gov-

---

* Appendix A.

ernments recognized the shell currency, so called, in their dealings with the Indians, and adopted it, to a certain extent, among themselves. From time to time, as the supply varied, they endeavored to fix its exchangeable value."

The colonists were obliged to adopt still other means of exchange, and, having no mints or banks, drew from such resources as they had. Thus among the commodities we find corn, meaning all kinds of grain, greatly used as currency, and live stock also received by the colonial treasury as "country pay" for taxes. Wool, beaver skins, codfish, and many other articles of every-day use, were allowed to pass current; musket-balls also at a farthing each, but no man was obliged to take more than twelvepence of them at one time. From the early records of the Massachusetts Colony, we find that these commodities were used in the payment of debts, and also recognized by the court as a proper penalty or fine to be administered by them.

It was a custom, when a surveyor ran the lines of a lot of land, to pay him with a peck of corn; and we find that "Sir Richard Saltonstall is fined four bushells of malte for his absence from Court."

This great variety of circulating medium, much of it in inconvenient form, and cargoes from the mother country, constantly draining the colony of the little specie it had, caused a great depression in trade. Land and commodities fell to one-half, and even to one-quarter, their first value. Merchants would take only money; and so it happened that men could not pay their debts, though considered as well off, and possessed of much property. Laws were enacted endeavoring to fix the value of various articles of currency, and the value of wampum was greatly enhanced. But the great scarcity of hard money caused embarrassment in every species of exchange; all confidence was destroyed. This state of things continued for a long time, and made much trouble. Governor Winthrop relates an incident of this period: "A master, being forced to sell a pair of his oxen to pay his servant his wages, told his servant he could keep him no longer, not knowing how to pay him next year. The servant answered him, he could serve him for more of his cattle. But what shall I do (saith the master) when all my cattle are gone? The servant replied, you shall then serve me, and so you may have your cattle again." *

Of the currency at this and earlier periods of the history of the Colonists, there are full and interesting particulars in Felt's "Historical Account of Massachusetts Currency."

1646. — It is here, at this distressed point in the history of the Massachusetts Colonists, that we find the first intimation of paper-money in this country, the special subject of this report.† Of such bills

---

* Winthrop, vol. i. p. 220.   † Appendix B.

we can at this time learn nothing definite, either in regard to their form or value: without doubt, however, they were issued by individuals, either merchants or traders. That there probably were such bills, we have some evidence; for, in 1646, there was an enactment that any person, forging notes of hand, or other paper relative to property, " shall stand in the pilory three seuerall lecture days and render double damages to the party wronged, and disabled to give any evidence or verdict to any Courte or Magistrate."* From this it would seem that such notes had been issued, and that forgery must be forbidden to protect the pecuniary interests of the people. Felt, in alluding to the formation of the mint, in 1652, says, that, " not satisfied with this means of obtaining an increased medium of circulation for the purposes of traffic, serious thoughts are entertained of resorting to paper money, *in addition to what had been already issued by individuals.*"

In the Appendix to Hull's Diary in the third volume of this Society's publications is an extract from an address prepared by the colonists to be presented to King Charles, in 1684, containing this passage, referring to the period of the formation of the mint, in 1652: " And as for the minting and stamping pieces of silver to pass amongst ourselves for xii*d.*, vi*d.*, iii*d.*, we were necessiated thereunto, having no

---

* Colony Laws, p. 155.

staple commodity in our country to pay debts or buy necessaries but fish and corn, which was so cumbersome and troublesome as could not be borne; and therefore for some yeares *paper bills* passed in payment of debts, which are very subject to be lost, rent, or counterfeited, and other inconveniences." Also in a report accepted by the Legislature is the following: "What hath bin thought of by any for raiseing a *Banke* or engaging in generall trade or relating to monies in regard to the badnesse of it, or highnesse or lownesse of it, with very many other matters tending to the promoting and well regulating of trades will by this means be ripened, and things reduced to a more comfortable state, than wee now find."* These bills or notes were probably not issued in large amounts, but as a convenience in the way of trade, and may perhaps be termed traders-notes, and were very likely received by the government in the payment of taxes, where the parties issuing them were known to be reliable.

1650. — In 1650, the colonists, finding that specie still continued very scarce by reason of the vigilance with which the English authorities prevented its exportation hither, and because the European merchants drew the little coin there was from the country, and the trade of the province increasing, especially with the West Indies, by which means large amounts of bul-

---

* Massachusetts Archives.

lion were brought in, they began to consider the expediency of establishing a mint.

1652. — As is well known, this was done in 1652, without authority from the home government; but no notice was taken of it by Cromwell or Parliament, nor was there, till some twenty years after, during the reign of Charles II., when a commission from England ordered the coinage to be stopped. But this order was not complied with, and it was not till 1685 that the coinage of the Massachusetts mint was suppressed.*

1675. — In 1675, after King Philip's war, specie was so scarce, and the want of it so pressing, that a mode approaching somewhat to a paper-currency was introduced. The Legislature enact, that, " for the prevention of the charge and trouble of transportation of the rates to be leveyed, to the Treasurer of the Country, as also a matter of convenience, therein appearing, It is ordered that bills for wages, horses, provisions, &c., being regularly passed to the sayd Treasurer, the Treasurer vpon the desire of persons concerned, shall repasse bills to the Constables of such Townes, where sums are due vpon the aforesaid accounts." †

1686. — There is evidence, also, that in 1686 a bank was formed by a gentleman of Boston, with

---

* The New-England shilling and sixpence, and what is known as the pine-tree money, were coined at this mint.
† Massachusetts Records.

several others, some from England, who were authorized to commence the issuing of bills, on the security of real and personal estate, in some respects similar to the Land Bank of twenty-eight years later; but we have so little record of its history, that no detailed or definite account of it can be given. From the Massachusetts Archives we find that authority was given to certain persons to start a bank and issue bills, in these words: "And having perused and considered a proposall, made to us by John Blackwell of Boston Esqr, on behalf of himself and divers others, his participants, as well in England as in this Countrey," liberty is granted for the Directors, or "conservatives" of the bank, to commence the issuing of bills, on real and personal security, and on merchandise. The writer of a pamphlet, entitled "A Letter from one in Boston To his Friend in the Country in answer to a Letter directed to John Burril Esqre 1714," says, "Our Fathers about Twenty-eight years ago, entered into a Partnership to circulate their Notes founded on Land Security, stamped on Paper, as our Province Bills, which gave no offence to the Government then, and that at a time, when the Prerogative of the Crown was extended further than ever has been since." From these statements it would seem that bills were issued in Massachusetts in 1686.

1690. — In 1690, however, the first public bills of credit were issued that were known in the American Colonies; and then began the reign of paper-money in this country, a reign not yet ended, as the financial records of the day so unpleasantly prove to us. These bills were issued just after the return of the troops from the disastrous expedition to Canada, undertaken by Massachusetts, in connection with New York and Connecticut.

Hutchinson says: "The government were utterly unprepared for the return of the forces. They seem to have presumed, not only upon success, but upon the enemy's treasure to bear the charge of the expedition." The soldiers became clamorous for their pay, and were nearly at the point of mutiny: some means must be adopted for paying them, and the government decided to issue paper-money. The General Court made a tax equal to the demand, and issued bills of credit with which they paid the public debt, and promised to receive the bills in discharge of the tax. A committee was empowered to make an immediate issue of seven thousand pounds, in bills from five shillings to five pounds. The whole amount of this emission, with the re-emissions up to 1702, amounted to about one hundred and ten thousand pounds, or five hundred and fifty thousand dollars; a small amount certainly, when compared with the circulation of the Massachusetts banks at the present time, which is, as appears by the late report of the Bank Commissioners, over fifty-two million dollars.

Bills of this issue are now extremely rare: we have

been able to hear of but two specimens, now in existence, which seem to be genuine. A notice of one of these we find in a late volume of the "Proceedings of the Massachusetts Historical Society." This bill was exhibited at a meeting of that Society, by its honored President, who alludes to its rarity, and says, " It is written with a pen, not engraved; and the seal of the Province is very inartistically drawn. One might almost suppose it to have been a mere draught of the design for the notes, rather than one of the notes themselves. But it is indented and signed and countersigned. The signatures are evidently original; and the bill is numbered 4980 on the face, and No. 62 on the back."

The Historical Society had a fac-simile of this bill prepared for their published volume, and we copy the reading of it therefrom: —

"No. (4980) 5 s

"THIS Indented bill of Five shillings due from the Massachusets Colony to the Possesor shall be in Value equal to money & shall be accordingly accepted by the Treasurer & receivers subordinate to him in all publick payments and for any Stock at any time in the Treasury — Boston in New-England December the 10th 1690: By order of ye General Court.

[Seal.]
Come over & help us.

JOHN PHILLIPS
ADAM WINTHROP } Com^{tee} *
PENN TOWNSEND

SIGILVM: GVB: & SOC^s
DE: MATTACHVSETS:
BAY IN: NOV: ANGL:"

---

* Appendix C.

In Drake's "History and Antiquities of Boston," we find a description of another bill of this issue, which differs from the preceding in not having the same signers, and being dated Feb. 3, 1690, instead of Dec. 10, 1690.* It would seem, that the date given by Mr. Drake, as on the bill described by him, must be incorrect, from the fact that the expedition to Canada, the failure of which caused the issue of these bills, did not leave Boston till August, 1690, six months after the apparent issue of the bill described by him. This seeming discrepancy, however, is to be explained by the fact, that, in legal documents of that time, the year did not legally end till March 25, the closing of the legislative year; so that this bill, although dated Feb. 3, 1690, was in fact issued in February, 1691. Drake says of these bills, they were struck from an engraved plate, upon pieces of paper nearly square, about five and three-fourths inches from top to bottom, and about five inches wide; the colony seal in the left-hand corner. It would seem strange, that so large an issue as seven thousand pounds, in bills of from five shillings to five pounds, should have been written by hand; the manual labor necessary to have prepared them must have been very great, besides the time it must have taken; and the unavoidable difference in the looks of the bills, when

---

* The signers, as given by Drake, were Elisha Hutchinson, John Wally, and Tim. Thornton.

prepared by different persons, as they would necessarily have to be, would be strong evidence that some other method was pursued. Drake speaks of the bill, which he describes, as being before him, and says it is from an engraved plate. It is almost impossible to decide which is the correct statement, without a careful examination of the bills. The number of these bills that were collected by the treasurer, and burned, would naturally cause them to be exceedingly rare; only such being saved as might have been accidentally laid aside till after the time of redemption had passed, or perhaps kept as a curiosity by some zealous antiquary. Hutchinson speaks of seeing, in 1749, a five-shilling bill, of the issue of 1690, in a manner which would indicate that even then they were not often seen. The bill exhibited to the Historical Society, however, bears such evident marks of being genuine, that we are led to suppose it was one of the first issued, and, in the anxiety of the government to pay off the troops at once, the bills were written, and not engraved. The art of engraving also was not practised to any extent in this country at that time, and it would have been difficult to have got the plates engraved in England in time to meet the exigency of the occasion. It is well known, that, in later years, plates for bills of credit were made in England.

These bills of 1690 were secured in a measure by

a tax, and were receivable for treasury dues, but were not then "in value equal to money," as stated on their face; for they would not buy goods at money rates or prices. Many of the soldiers lost heavily on them, and could not get more than twelve or fourteen shillings a pound for them. As the time for payment of taxes came near, they increased in value; and in 1692 it was ordered by the Court, "that all bills of publik creditt, issued forth by order of ye Generall Court of ye late Colony of ye Massachusetts Bay, shall pass current within this Province in all payments equivalent to money, and in all publick payments at 5 per cent. advance. And for encouragement to such persons as are possessors of said Bills, to lend them for ye service of ye publick, it is further enacted that they shall be secured by ye publick Taxes and other Revenues, and shall be reimburst in money within twelve months."* After this, owing to the five per cent bonus, they became worth more than hard money when the time for the payment of the taxes arrived, and for twenty years or more they did not depreciate much below silver. This first emission of legal-tender bills in this country was finally drawn in, without any bad influence upon the whole currency. It was a short time previous to the passage of this Act that Sir William Phipps was said to have come forward, and exchanged

---

* Appendix D.

his own coin for a large amount of this paper-currency at par, in order, if possible, to restore confidence to the public.

1691. — In 1691, it was ordered that the bills out and to be emitted shall not exceed forty thousand pounds. Of this sum ten thousand pounds was drawn in and burnt in October, 1691. In the following years no more new emissions but remissions of the remainder, and, only for the charges of government, called in by rates or taxes within the year: the last re-emission of these bills was nine thousand pounds, in 1701. Bills of this period continued at the rate of six shillings a heavy piece of eight, and were called Old-Charter bills, because they were issued before the second Charter of William and Mary.

1702. — In 1702, the first year of Queen Anne's reign, there was another emission of ten thousand pounds; and, during the war of Queen Anne, the government issued bills annually, to be cancelled by the taxes of the same and the following year, until 1704.* A rare pamphlet upon the subject of paper-money, says of the issue of these bills, "Which not being very considerable, and the bills having a preference in the Treasury to silver, kept up their credit until about the year 1711, when such large sums were issued that silver began to be hoarded by some, and

---

* Appendix E.

exported by others in large quantities, and the bills became the only means and instrument by which private trade and dealing were regulated and managed. And to confine the currency of the bills, and effectually to banish silver and gold, the Massachusetts Province, in the year 1712, made their bills a tender in the discharge of all debts, unless there appeared a special agreement or contract otherwise." *

1704. — In 1704, as well as in times past, the Colonists were much troubled by the counterfeiting of the bills of credit; and the General Court, from time to time, enacted laws in relation to it. We find the following enactment, in the records of the Court for this year: —

" Some ill disposed and wicked Persons, designing the hurt of this Province, and of Her Majesties good Subjects within the same and for base lucre and gain to themselves, have forged and uttered several Counterfeit Bills, in imitation of the Twenty Shilling Bills of Credit on this Province, thereby Imposing a Vile Cheat and Cousenage on some less discerning and unwary Persons," it was enacted that such persons upon being convicted were to be punished, " in such manner as is by law provided against Forgery, and be branded in the right cheek with a hot Iron with the Letter F." They were also to pay double dam-

---

* "A Brief Account of the Rise, Progress, and Present State of the Paper Currency of New England." Boston, 1749.

ages to the person known to be defrauded by such false bills. Some such enactment might not be out of place at the present day, defrauded and imposed upon as the public now are by the counterfeiting of the paper-currency.

In 1714, counterfeiting had increased to such an extent, that it was enacted by the Court, "that every person convicted of falsifying, Forging, or Counterfeiting any of the Bills of Credit on this Province, should be deemed and adjudged a Felon, and suffer the pains of Death as in case of Felony; any Law, Usage or Custom to the Contrary notwithstanding."

It also became necessary to make similar regulations to those imposed by the Treasury Department at the present day in relation to the torn and defaced currency in circulation. The treasurer of the Colony was not allowed to receive any torn bills, unless the possessor made oath that they were torn or defaced while in his hands.

1713. — Among the bills of credit in the possession of the Society, we find one which appears to have been authorized by the General Court, in October, 1713; but we have not been able to find any record of the enactment in the volumes of the Colonial Laws in our library. This bill is signed by A. Winthrop, A. Davenport, Wm. Payne, and Saml. Checkley. From the dates on the margin, it must have been printed from a plate prepared for re-emis-

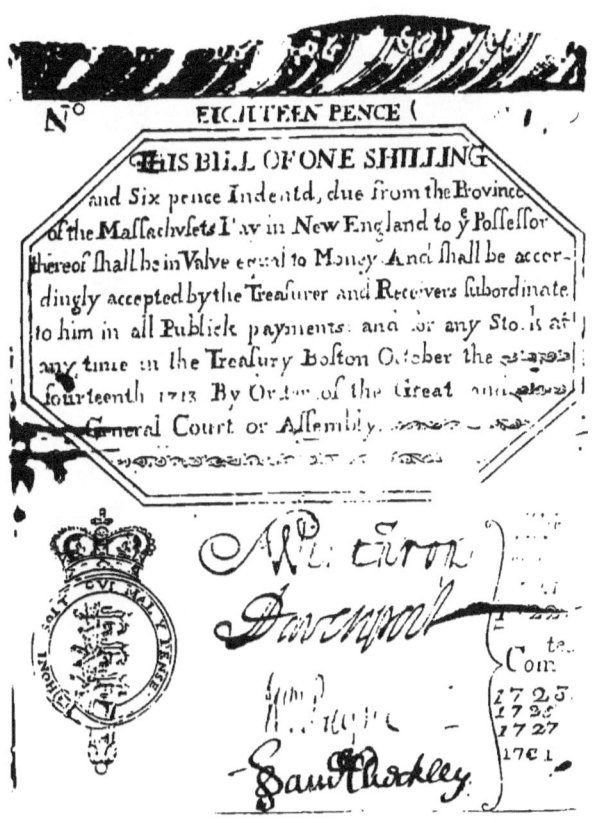

Specimen of a Massachusetts Bill issued under the Act of 1713. Photographed from an original bill in possession of the American Antiquarian Society.

sion, it being customary to engrave upon the plate the year of each re-emission. On this bill are nine dates, besides the date of 1713 in the body of it: the last date is 1731, at which time this bill was probably issued.*

1714. — In 1714, there was a cry of great scarcity of money, and the public mind was harassed to devise some remedy for the evils under which the Colony was laboring. Of course there was a great diversity of opinion: some were in favor of abolishing paper entirely, and having specie only as a circulating medium; others wanted a private bank based on real estate; and a third party approved a system of loaning by the Province to the people, on interest.

Controversies arose on these opinions, and spread their influence through towns and families. Pamphlets and letters (several of which are in our library †) were published by one party, reflecting upon the judgment and motives of another, who advocated a different plan. The whole colony was agitated to discover some remedy for the difficulties that the trading community labored under. The first party, which was for depending upon specie entirely and abolishing paper, and of which Mr. Hutchinson was one, was very small. The second, from a project pub-

---

* Appendix F.
† See list of books and pamphlets in Appendix.

lished in 1684, in London, had taken up the scheme of a private bank, based upon real estate to a sufficient amount, as security. The London scheme not being generally known, a Boston merchant received the authorship of it. This scheme by its opponents was stigmatized in various pamphlets as "South Sea Buble," "Pandora's Box," and as an infringement of the royal prerogative, and covering a design for absolute power. But in a "Vindication" published in 1714, the writer says, the gentlemen interested, "after several meetings, agreed upon a Land Security as a Fund for Bills and Notes to be Circulated, and minutes were then drawn up, for the Regulating and carrying on that Affair, but all with an intire dependance upon the Government for their Favour and Countenance in promoting it, and furnishing them with all necessary Powers as might enable them to carry it on with safety to themselves, and the Possessors of their Bills or Notes." Some members of the Government apparently approved of the plan, so they proceeded "to mutually covenant, consent, and agree as follows: —

"1. That the subscriptions shall be taken to a value not exceeding £300,000, and that every subscriber shall settle and make over a Real Estate, to the value of his Respective Subscription, to the Trustees of the Partnership or Bank, to be and remain as a Fund or Security for such Bills as shall be Emitted therefrom; which Emission shall not exceed the Subscription, and will make good all deficiencies that shall arise from any Neglect Default or Mismanagement of any of the Officers or Members of this Partnership or Bank.

"2. That no Person shall Subscribe above Four Thousand Pounds, nor under Two Hundred and Fifty Pounds; and each Subscriber shall take out and keep for two years at least, one quarter part of his Subscription, and not exceed one half part by virtue of his first Mortgage, paying interest therefor, acording to the Rules of this Partnership.

"3. That we will from time to time, and at all times for ever hereafter give Credit to the Bills Emitted from this Fund or Bank, equal to what is given to the Bills of Credit on the Province of the Massacusetts Bay, and to accept the said Bills in all Payments, (Specialties and Obligations for any other Specie excepted) upon Forfeiture of Fifty Pounds for each refusal, until the Refuser has forfeited his whole Security and Profits; and every such Person having so forfeited, shall no longer be accounted a Member of this Partnership, but be deemed *ipso facto* dismist, and Lose his Interest therein."

Another section authorized the emitting of bills of credit upon good security, at certain rates and values, " On Wooden Houses without Farms, not exceeding the Value of the Lands belonging to them." Also on brick houses, " on Gold not exceeding Five Pounds Ten Shillings per Ounce;" and on silver, iron, and other imperishable articles, at fixed rates, according to the market.

Section 19 provided that, "when there shall be Emitted and Continued at Interest One Hundred and Fifty Thousand Pounds," certain sums should be given out of the net profits, " to the use of an Hospital or Charity School, for the Support and Education of the poor Children in the Town of Boston," also to Harvard College for specified purposes, &c., &c.*

---

* Appendix G.

They chose as their motto, "Crescit Eundo." The form of their bills was to be as follows: —

"This Indented Bill of Credit, obliges us, and every of us, and all, and every of our Partners of the Bank of Credit of Boston in New England, to accept the same in lieu of Twenty Shillings, in all Payments, according to our Articles of Agreement; and that it shall be so accepted by our Receiver or Treasurer, for the Redemption of any Pawn or Mortgage in the said Bank.

"Boston, November First, One Thousand Seven Hundred and Fourteen."

The voice of the people was loud and vehement for more money; and the government, fearing the success of the "Land Bank," as it was called, issued an order, which the projectors construed as an encouragement to proceed and perfect their scheme and subscriptions, for the inspection of the Council. But, while they were thus promoting their interests, the party for a public bank prevailed, and gained a loan of fifty thousand pounds in bills of credit, which were put into the hands of trustees, and lent for five years to any of the inhabitants, at five per cent interest.* This effectually defeated the "Land-Bank" project for the time being, but it was not fully conquered. They did not, however, as far as can be ascertained, ever issue any of their bills: for, of course, after the establishment of the public bank, they could not get the sanction of government; and so, necessarily, complied with the order of the Court, and never emitted any

---

* Appendix H.

bills; or presented their scheme. Attorney-General Dudley had strenuously opposed this scheme for a " Land Bank," thereby receiving great opposition from those interested in its success; and he prepared a pamphlet on the subject, which was published anonymously.* This called out the "Vindication" before alluded to.

From this time (1714) onward, the country was for many years divided on the question of a public or private bank. The mercantile part of the community were still discontented with the inadequacy of the government loan; and a petition from some eighty Boston gentlemen was sent in for a more extended issue, or larger medium of trade. After Governor Dudley's removal, in 1715, and Mr. Shute's arrival, the latter advised, in his first speech, that an attempt should be made to revive the low state of trade. The House took this as an intimation that he would sanction another Treasury loan. Accordingly, December 4, 1716, another loan of a hundred thousand pounds was issued, which was secured by mortgaged estates, of double the value of the sum borrowed, for ten years, at five per cent annually. The profits were to pay expenses of the government, and bills were to be returned and burnt at the expiration of the time fixed. The result of this emission was to depreciate the currency still more. Some of this

---

* Objections to the Bank of Credit lately projected at Boston, &c.

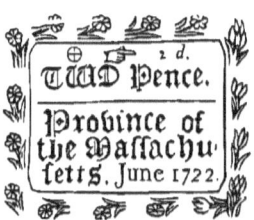

Fac-simile of the One and Two-penny Bills issued by the Colony of Massachusetts Bay, in 1722, from the originals on parchment in the possession of the American Antiquarian Society.

five hundred pounds' worth of small bills, or, as we now call it, fractional currency, were ordered. Among the earliest specimens of paper-money in the possession of this Society are two bills of this issue: they are of the denomination of one and two pennies, and are exceedingly rare. We have been able, after much inquiry of collectors and others, to hear of but one other genuine bill of this issue, which is said to be in the possession of a gentleman of Salem. The bills were printed on parchment, and each denomination was different in form; the one-penny being round, the two-penny nearly square, and the three-penny piece sexangular. As has been stated, this emission was for only five hundred pounds; consequently the issue was soon drawn in, or so badly torn and disfigured as to become, like some of the currency of the present day, wholly unrecognizable as money. The act issuing these bills was as follows:—

"An Act for Emitting Five Hundred Pounds in ſmall Bills of ſeveral Denominations, to be exchanged for larger Bills by the Province Treaſurer.

"Whereas great Inconveniences and Difficulties have ariſen to the Affairs of Trade of this Province for want of ſmall money for change:

"For remedy whereof Be it enacted by His Excellency the Governour, Council and Repreſentatives in General Court aſſembled, and by the Authority of the Same, That there be forthwith Imprinted on Parchment the ſum of Five Hundred Pound in Pennies, Two Pences and Three Pences of the following Figure, and Inſcriptions: viz. Forty Thouſand and One Pennies, to be Round, Twenty Thouſand Two Pences, Four Square, Thirteen Thouſand Three Hundred and Thirty,—three pences ſex-angular.

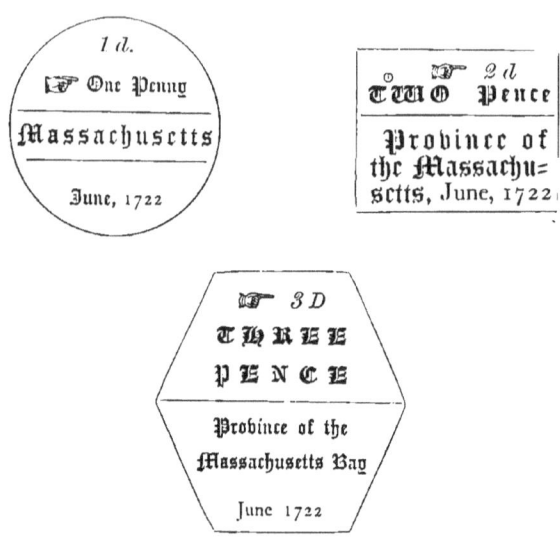

"And that the Committee already appointed by the Court for that purpofe are hereby Directed and Impowered to take Effectual Care for the making and Imprinting faid Bills; and that the faid bills be delivered to the Treafurer of the Province by him to be exchanged for other Bills of this Province, to such perfons as come for the fame; but not lefs than Twenty Shillings at any one time; and that the Bills be accepted by the Treafurer and Receivers fubordinate to him in all Publick Payments, as other the Bills of this Province are, and that Five Hundred Pounds in Bills Exchanged by the Treafurer for thefe Bills, fhall be burnt to afhes by a Committee to be appointed for that purpose."

1728. — In March, 1728, the paper-money of Massachusetts in circulation amounted to three hundred and fourteen thousand pounds, in addition to the bills of Rhode Island, Connecticut, and New Hampshire,

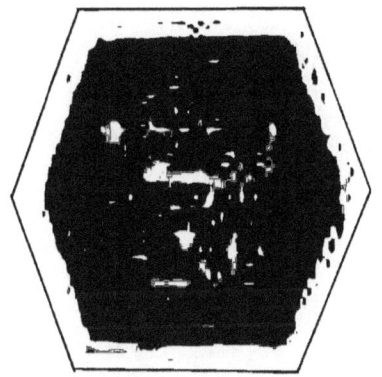

then in circulation in the colony. Large amounts of the currency from these colonies was in circulation in Massachusetts, and strong efforts were made by the Boston merchants to prevent its circulation. Silver went up from nineteen shillings to twenty-seven shillings the ounce, and continued about the same rate for several years.

1730. — In 1730, when the pecuniary state of the Province was in this condition, Jonathan Belcher succeeded to the chief magistracy. Of him, the Court of St. James had great hope that he would be able to subdue the refractory spirit of Massachusetts, and make a speedy close to the issuing of paper-money: so he came with authority to effect this in ten years. The injunctions of His Majesty restricted the issues of Treasury notes to be limited to cancelling government charges, and not more than thirty thousand pounds to be in circulation at the same time.

1733. — In 1733, the merchants and others of Boston, finding the Treasury curtailed, attempted to supply the deficiency, by engaging in a project for issuing paper to the value of one hundred and ten thousand pounds. These bills were to be redeemable in two years, with silver at the common rate of Province paper, which was, at this time, nineteen shillings an ounce. These merchants' notes circulated, and were even considered better than the Province Bills, owing to the provision making them redeemable in silver.

It is not our purpose, nor would it be possible within the limits of this Report, to speak in detail of *all* the emissions of bills by the Massachusetts Colony, but only to allude as briefly as possible to such issues as we may have specimens of in our collection, and to any important epoch in the history of the paper-money of the Colony.

1737. — In the collection of this Society is a poor and very imperfect specimen of a bill of three shillings, issued in 1737. It is one of the emission of eighteen thousand pounds, authorized by the General Court to be recalled in one year; and a sinking fund was made for this amount, the people being allowed to pay their taxes in hemp and flax, at certain rates, or in hard or paper money, as they desired. In the same year, nine thousand pounds were issued, redeemable in five years, and these bills were called new tenor; the others, old tenor. This last issue was not receivable in payment of the duties of "Impost and Tunnage of shipping;" they being payable in hard money, as in the present day. In many particulars, the legal-tender notes of this day are not unlike these bills of credit of a hundred and twenty-nine years ago: our greenbacks, although a legal tender, are not receivable for duties on importations.

In July of 1737, an act was passed by the General Court, authorizing the issue of two thousand six hundred and twenty-five pounds in small bills of several

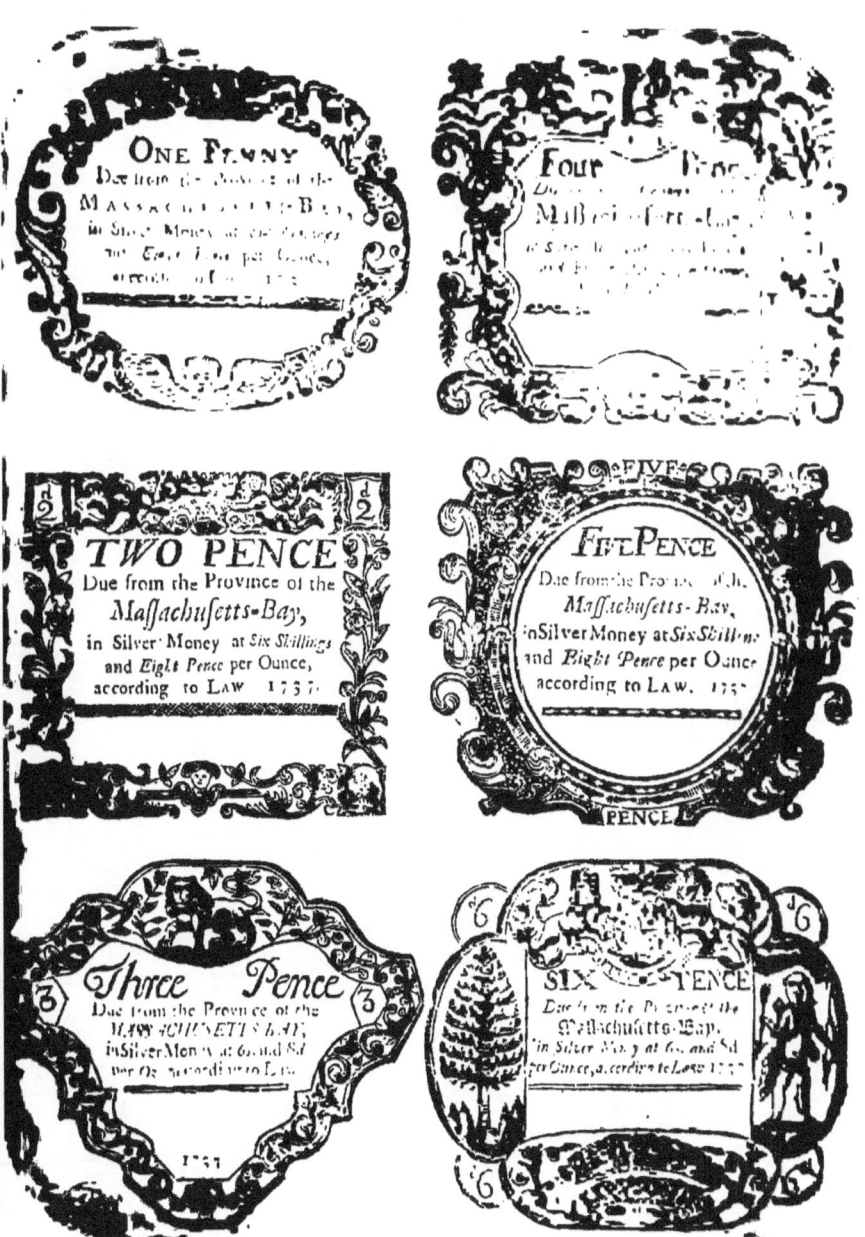

Specimen of the small bills issued by Massachusetts in 1737. Photographed from book of Colonial Laws.

denominations, to be exchanged for larger bills by the Province Treasury. These bills were to be of the denomination of one penny, twopence, threepence, fourpence, fivepence, and sixpence. In the publication of the acts of the General Court for 1737 are illustrations representing the form of these small bills. There are probably none of them in existence now.*

1739. — In 1739, there was a general dread of the drawing-in of all the paper-money, without any substitute for it; for it was known that most of the coin had been driven out of the country by the bad management of the currency. Thomas Hutchinson, at that time a prominent member of the General Court, then laid a scheme before the government for borrowing from England, upon interest, a sum in silver equal to all the bills then extant, — of which there were two hundred and ten thousand pounds in circulation, forty thousand pounds on loan, and the remainder to be brought into the Treasury in 1742; therewith to redeem them from the possessors, and thus furnish a currency for the country: the silver was to be paid at distant periods. But his scheme was rejected, and private persons resolved to interpose, as royal instructions were no bar to the proceedings of private individuals; so far had the colony, in spirit, established its independence. Thus it was that the Land-Bank, or Manufactory Scheme of 1714, came to be revived, and produced such great and lasting mischief. The pro-

---

* Appendix I.

jector of that bank now put himself at the head of seven or eight hundred persons, says Hutchinson (Felt says three hundred and ninety-five), " some, men of mark and good estate, but generally of small means; and some were insolvent." This company were to lend one hundred and fifty thousand pounds, lawful money, on land security, and payable in twenty years by merchandise or produce.

The Directors and a Treasurer were chosen by the Company, and each partner was to pay three per cent of the sum taken out, and five per cent of the principal; and he who did not pay bills might pay in produce and manufactures at the rate determined from time to time by the Directors. The fate of the project was thought to depend upon its reception by the General Court; therefore they wanted the Representatives well disposed. The needy part of the Province favored the scheme, and they were most numerous: so it appeared that the majority of Representatives for the year 1740 were subscribers, or favorers of the scheme; and the popular branch of the General Court for that year has since been called the "Land-Bank House." Men of property and the principal merchants violently opposed this scheme, and would not receive its bills; but large numbers of the shopkeepers took them. Another scheme to lessen the temptation to take Land-Bank bills was that of Edward Hutchinson and one hundred and six partners, for one hundred and twenty thousand pounds to be redeemed in fifteen years, with silver at twenty shillings per ounce, and gold *pro rata;* much like the scheme of 1733. The bills were called "merchants' notes;" and this scheme was promoted to put down the other, though it also was considered inexpedient, but, being on a specie basis, was less objectionable than the Land or Manufactory Bank. Governor Belcher was greatly opposed to the Land Bank, and exerted himself to the utmost to defeat this fraudulent enterprise, but was wholly unable to do it; the majority of the inhabitants of the Province being in favor of it. At length, application was made to Parliament for an act to suppress it, which was very readily obtained: so the Company was dissolved, but the act gave the possessors of the bills a right of action against any Director for the sum expressed, with interest. The Company were amazed, but met for some action to endeavor to redeem their notes. Many of the bills had not been issued for the value expressed, and many possessors had acquired them for half their value; so justice could not be done to all. For the Company it was considered a just judgment for their unwarrantable proceedings. It was thus that many wealthy families were reduced to poverty, and but few escaped unharmed. If Parliament had not interposed, there would have been great confusion in the Province in this matter, and governmental authority would have been in the Land-Bank Company. The Legislature put the concerns of the bank into the hands of commissioners to be brought to a close; but nearly thirty years elapsed before that was fully accomplished, and many of the commissioners did not live to complete the service.

It was of this bank that Samuel Adams, Esq., father of the patriot, was a Director; and after his death, in 1747, his estate, then in the possession of his son, was advertised by the sheriff of Suffolk County to be sold at auction to pay a claim against the Land Bank.* The future Governor did not, however, give up the property; having, as Hutchinson says, threatened the officer if he undertook to make the sale, and also intimidated any person who was desirous of purchasing. There is evidence, however, that means were taken by the friends of Mr. Adams to pay the claim, and that a subscription was started for that purpose, signed by John Hancock, James Pitts, Joseph Warren, and others, by which the sum of one thousand pounds, and over, was raised to pay the claim, so that no threats were necessary on the part of Mr. Adams to enable him to retain his property. †

From "The Life and Public Services of Samuel Adams," by William V. Wells, we take the following in relation to the Land Bank: "Memorials of their transactions, found in the public records, show that the bank was in successful operation in October and November, 1741, — when Samuel Adams, Esq., and others of the Directors, appear as the grantors of a

---

* Appendix J.
† Historical and Genealogical Register.

certain parcel of land, for the sum of forty pounds, to Eliphlet Pond, yeoman; and, subsequently, Messrs. Robert Auchmuty, Samuel Adams, and others acknowledge the receipt of twenty pounds, 'in bills called Manufactory Bills,' from one Kingman, which releases him from the mortgage to that amount on his estate, and the interest, two pound nine shillings and threepence, paid."

Mr. M. W. Stickney, of Salem, has in his possession one of these mortgage-deeds, given by John Spofford, of Rowley, on his farm, for the sum of one hundred pounds in "Bills of Credit called Manufactory Bills;" also the release of the Directors of the Company, signed by George Leonard, Samuel Adams, Thomas Cheever, John Choate, and Robert Hale, bearing date April 22, 1742. These records of the Land-Bank Company give us some idea of the nature of their operations.

When Governor Belcher, in endeavoring to suppress the Land Bank, issued a proclamation that all commissioned officers who had encouraged this scheme should be dismissed from office, Samuel Adams (senior) and John Choate sent a communication to the Governor, stating that, as holding a commission under his Excellency was inconsistent with prosecuting the manufactory scheme, they do now, "with your Excellency's leave, resign these trusts." Robert Hale, of Beverly, another of the Directors, also resigned his commission; and William Stoddard and

William Watts, of Boston, had their commissions as justices nullified by the General Court, for favoring such an association. Among the letters of those who fell under the Governor's displeasure was one from Henry Lee, of Worcester, in which he declares himself an approver of the manufactory scheme, and says, " I am determined to do what I can to encourage it, and think the privilege of an Englishman is my sufficient warrant. To sacrifice my post for the service of my country is infinitely more honorable than to keep it on such base conditions." * Here we have an early spark of the revolutionary spirit.

1740. — In 1740, another sum of one hundred and twenty thousand pounds was emitted on a silver basis, to overwhelm the Land Bank. The sponsors for this amount were eminent, wealthy merchants.

The bills of the Land Bank were to be paid in twenty years in goods at an arbitrary price.

It would have been a light burden to the inhabitants to have paid the charges upon every year, and the debt for that year besides; but, instead, the government let year after year pass with light taxes, and heavily burdened more distant years. Thus, 1741, the last year, came to have a heavy weight of debt upon it; and, though it was far short of what had been paid the four or five preceding years, it was

---

* Henry Lee was one of the early settlers of Worcester, Mass., to whom were assigned thirty acres of land; and who complied with the order of the Court, to erect a house thereon.

deemed an insupportable burden. It was thought that the government order for calling in the bills that year would be openly violated in some way; any such explosion or rebellion was prevented, by Governor Belcher being superseded before the period arrived.

Governor Belcher was misrepresented, by those who favored the Land Bank, to the Royal Council; and he was dismissed from his office.

1741. — William Shirley was in July, 1741, appointed his successor to take up his work. He did not insist on withdrawing the Province notes as soon as his predecessor did, but wished a committee of the court to meet at Milton to examine the state of the Land Bank. They found that about forty-nine thousand pounds of its notes had been struck off and endorsed; the Treasurer had issued the amount of thirty-five thousand pounds; and the Directors were using four thousand pounds in trade. After this the transactions of the Company were greatly restricted.*

1742. — The Equity Bill was enacted in January, 1742, which required "that, after the first of February next, all coined silver of sterling alloy shall pass as lawful, at 6s. 8d. the ounce, troy weight; and other money in the same proportion." It provided that debts contracted within five years should be payable in bills of credit at the above rate or proportion, unless by special agreement otherwise; and, if they depreciated, allowance to be made accordingly. In

---
* Appendix K.

March of the same year, a committee for settling the affairs of the Land Bank issued a call to its stockholders to settle the demands upon them; and, in April, the Governor published an Act of Parliament, which laid an interdict on all stock companies without charters. This led to a resolve, that, "whereas it is expedient and necessary for the peace and quiet of His Majesty's subjects in this Province, that all the notes of the silver and manufactory schemes should be drawn in and consumed, as soon as may be." A committee was appointed to investigate and report to that end. This committee report, that the "Silver-Scheme" association had emitted one hundred and twenty thousand pounds in notes, of which sixty-nine thousand three hundred and sixty-one pounds, twelve shillings, and sixpence, had been recalled, leaving still in circulation fifty thousand six hundred and thirty-eight pounds, seven shillings, and sixpence.

While the public mind was so much occupied with these banking institutions, the last issue of Province bills did not help the community so much as was desired. These notes, being payable in specie, were hoarded up, and others for produce and manufactures put forward; so that at last there were not enough of the Province notes to pay the taxes, and the currency of the adjoining colonies became the common one. Large amounts of bills from the colonies of Rhode Island and Connecticut were in circulation, so that the Massachusetts Colony was flooded with paper-money. A law against receiving the bills of adjacent colonies, unless they were redeemable in specie, was passed in 1739; but at this time, 1744, they were still received by many of the traders, and another bill was passed to prevent their circulation.

1745. — In 1745, the pressure on the Treasury was so great, that the government adopted the doubtful plan of a lottery, and tried to raise seven thousand five hundred pounds in this way, to meet the demands of the French war. One of the conditions of this concern was, "that whoever adventures thirty shillings in it may pay this sum, one-fifth in the new tenor, or in old-tenor bills at four for one; and the other four-fifths, in the same paper, or in any of New England, not prohibited."

1748. — In January, 1748, Mr. Kilby, our agent in London, wrote, that then there were many schemes before Parliament for having the colonial notes redeemed or recalled; and the Governor in his speech earnestly recommended to the Assembly, that they find some other way to supply the Treasury than by making new emissions of paper-money. In accordance with this advice, Thomas Hutchinson proposed, that the public notes be redeemed by the specie to be received from the Royal Exchequer, for the charges incurred in the capture of Louisburg. This proposition was coldly received at first; but, finally, gladly accepted, for the General Court were wearied by the Treasury-system of loans.

The other New-England colonies were consulted on the subject of redeeming the paper-currency; but they did not favor having a hard currency: the weight of depreciation in their notes had not fallen so heavily upon them as upon the Massachusetts Colony. Massachusetts persevered in her plan, however, and made a law for the redemption of all Province bills, requiring them to be exchanged at the Treasury before March 31, 1750, at certain rates which the law proceeds to fix; and a penalty was affixed for taking paper bills of the other colonies. Such a law was frequently renewed as a preventive until the Revolution.

1749. — In September, 1749, the "Evening Post," of Boston, announces the arrival of the specie paid by the Crown, in care of Mr. Bollan, our agent in London. This money consisted of six hundred and fifty-three thousand ounces of silver, and ten tons of copper : and there is good reason to believe it was the largest amount of specie ever in Massachusetts before, at one time ; thus it received the name of the "hard-money colony." *

1750. — In January, 1750, it was proposed, that three thousand pounds of small bills should be printed of one penny, twopence, threepence, fourpence halfpenny, sixpence, ninepence, and eighteen-pence, to prevent farthings and coined silver and gold

---

* Felt's Mass. Currency.

from passing at a proportionally higher rate than a milled dollar at six shillings. This was accepted.

1751. — In June, 1751, the Commissioners, appointed to redeem the public notes with specie, closed their labors, having redeemed £1,792,236, at the rate of one in specie to ten in paper. This was nearly all that was out, though, for years, parcels of them were found in old desks, the bottoms of leather chairs, and other private places, and brought in with a petition that they might be redeemed. The large number of these bills redeemed explains the great rarity of the colonial paper-money at the present day, and the reason we have so few specimens in our collection. A medium of exchange was still wanted, and Mr. Phips consented to issue Treasury notes, for money borrowed for the Province on interest; and, though it was not legal tender, it passed in special agreements, and was emitted till the Revolution, when it was renewed under a different administration.

1759. — In 1759, the Land-Bank question again came before the Legislature; and it was stated, that, nothwithstanding several laws had been passed to close it up, yet the affairs were still unsettled. Several of the partners had died, others had left the Province; and their bills were still out and unredeemed to the amount of nearly one thousand pounds. It was then voted, that the Commissioners, to pay their claims, assess three thousand pounds on any of the responsible partners, and, if they decline to pay the claims with interest in thirty days, to issue executions against them.

1760. — In 1760, the stockholders of the Land Bank petitioned for authority to start a lottery, to raise funds to meet the demands against them; and, there being much sympathy with them, the request was granted. Among the signers of this petition were Samuel Adams, William Stoddard, and Robert Auchmuty. This scheme was not very successful: only about six hundred pounds, out of the three thousand pounds wanted, was raised by it. Felt states, that "one great means of prolonging the settlement of this association's affairs was the loss of most of their records, with those of the Legislature, in 1747."

1767. — In 1767, the unfortunate Land-Bank question again made its appearance in the Legislature, and the Commissioners reported on their efforts to close up its affairs. What the final action on the matter was, we are unable to state, as the records of the General Court on the subject do not definitely record it. Probably the last claims — which in 1768, for principal and interest, amounted to about fifteen hundred pounds — were settled in some way by the Directors or their heirs. As will be seen by the statements already made, this scheme occasioned a bitter strife in politics, caused much legislation and prosecution, and was a source of great anxiety and loss to all connected, or directly concerned in it.

It is to be regretted that this Society have no specimens of the Land-Bank bills, and that there are probably but a few now in existence. It is to be hoped, however, that some antiquary who possesses them may see this statement, and be pleased to furnish our collection with a specimen of the bills issued by this company.

1772. — In 1772, paper-money of New York, New Jersey, and Nova Scotia, besides that of the other New-England colonies, was still in circulation in Massachusetts; and stringent laws were made to prevent its passing.

1774. — In 1774, the differences between Parliament and this colony had risen to so high a pitch as to indicate a speedy appeal to arms; but the finances were in an unusually good condition. Governor Hutchinson notices this fact, and says, "There never has been a time since the first settlement of the Country, when the Treasury has been in so good a state as it now is."

1775. — In May, 1775, when the condition of affairs was still more exciting, and hostilities had already commenced between the colonies and the adherents to the crown, it was ordered by the Committee of Safety appointed by the Provincial Congress, in consideration of the friendship displayed by our brethren of the colonies of Connecticut and Rhode Island in this time of public distress, in which all are so deeply interested, that their paper-currencies, which of late have been interdicted, be paid and received in the same proportion to silver as the same are paid and received within their respective colonies. And now began another issue of paper-money by Massachusetts, nearly like that issued years before, and also occasioned by war. Though this issue was under a very different authority, the expression of the bills was retained, lest the Royal Government might possibly withdraw from its purposes of compulsion.

An issue of bills, called soldiers' notes, was made at this time, not to exceed twenty-six thousand pounds, in various denominations from six to twenty shillings, which were made a legal tender, and were to be received for all payments due the Treasury.*

The Revolutionary authorities became aware that it would be necessary to raise large sums of money; and that, as there was a great uncertainty as to the result of the contest, the people would be backward in subscribing to a loan. Accordingly, the Provincial Congress made a stirring appeal to the people to come forward, and take up the loan, and thus sustain them in their efforts to maintain their rights. They say in their address to the people, "If you should furnish the money that is now needed, you will perform a meritorious service for your country, and prove yourselves sincerely attached to its interests; but, if an undue caution should prevent your doing this

---

* For description of the soldiers' notes, see Felt's "Mass. Currency."

essential service to the colony, the total loss both of your liberties and that very property — which you, by retaining it, affect to serve — may be the unhappy consequences."

The amount called for was one hundred thousand pounds, which was promptly taken up by our patriotic ancestors; and, although at great pecuniary loss to individuals, was of incalculable benefit to the country. Eighty-six years later, their descendants in Massachusetts proved their patriotism by a similar response to a call for money, to aid the Government in preserving the union of the country, which had come down to them through so much trial and tribulation.

1775. — It was in June, 1775, that the first Continental paper-currency was issued, according to resolutions of the Continental Congress, passed May 10th of the same year. In July, Massachusetts made the first issue of the noted "Sword-in-hand money," so called from the figure of an American on the back of each bill, with a drawn sword in his right hand.* We find in the collection of the Society several of these bills of different denominations and dates; but many of them are torn and disfigured.†

1776. — We have also specimens of the issues of 1776 and 1778, those of the latter year having a pine

---

* Appendix L.
† These bills were engraved by Paul Revere, an ingenious artist, and a worthy patriot.

tree engraved upon the back. In 1779, besides the tree on the back, there was an engraving of the rising sun on the face of the bill: of these, we have several good specimens.*

1780. — In 1780, under Congressional instructions, Massachusetts issued bills payable in six years, with interest at the rate of five per cent per annum. These bills had upon the back the guarantee of the United States to insure the payment of principal and interest. Of these bills, there are several fine specimens owned by the society: they are signed by R. Cranch and T. Dawes.†

The period of the redemption of this issue was put off so far, that the people had little confidence in it; and it rapidly depreciated to sixty for one of specie. There was also great dissatisfaction in the army against it, and recruits from Massachusetts could not be obtained, except by the promise of payment in hard money. In May, 1781, the Continental currency had depreciated to five hundred for one of hard money. The following extract from "Rivington's Gazette" of May 12, 1781, shows how low the estimate of paper-money was at this time: "The Congress is finally bankrupt. Last Saturday, a large body of the inhabitants, with paper-dollars in their hats by way of cockades, paraded the streets of Philadelphia,

---

* John Gill, one of the publishers of the "Boston Evening Gazette," printed the Massachusetts bills of 1776.

† Appendix L.

carrying colors flying, with a *dog tarred;* and, instead of the usual appendage and ornament of feathers, his back was covered with the Congress paper-dollars. This example of disaffection, immediately under the eyes of the rulers of the revolted Provinces in solemn session at the State-house assembled, was directly followed by the jailor, who refused accepting the bills in purchase of a glass of rum; and afterwards by the traders of the city, who shut up their shops, declining to sell any more goods but for gold or silver. It was declared also by the popular voice, that, if the opposition to Great Britain was not in future carried on by solid money instead of paper bills, all further resistance to the mother-country was in vain, and must be given up."* Although these statements of Rivington, who was a strong tory, are to be taken with some degree of doubt as to their entire truth, still it is an indication of the feeling of many of the people in regard to the Continental currency.

It is not proposed in this paper to speak in detail of the Revolutionary issues of paper-money by the United States or Massachusetts, as the currency issued, by the authority of Congress and by the States, at this period, became so connected and interwoven with each other, that to give a true history of one would require an examination into the whole system of the finances. This would be too lengthy a subject

---

* Diary of the Revolution.

for the limits of this Report; but, owing to the larger number of bills of this time being in existence, more attention has been drawn to them, and their history is more generally known.

We conclude these remarks with a brief allusion to the beginning of the present system of banks, authorized by the General Government, or by the States.

The first Bank of Discount and Deposit, of which we have record, was established in Venice, in the year 1171; and was founded in time of war, when the Republic fell short of funds, and had to adopt some expedient to sustain itself: although not at first issuing bills, in the course of time a method approximating to it was adopted. The Great Council decided upon raising a forced loan; and every citizen was obliged to contribute the one-hundredth part of his possessions, upon interest at the rate of five per cent. This bank, or chamber of loans, as it might perhaps more correctly be called, was originated for the purpose of managing this public debt.[*]

1781. — Six hundred and ten years after the formation of the bank at Venice, in the year 1781, and also in time of war, the first bank in the United States, authorized by Congress, was founded at Philadelphia, and called the Bank of North America. This bank was started with a capital of four hun-

---

[*] "Bankers' Magazine," 1857.

dred thousand dollars, and is in existence at the present day, as a national bank, with a capital of one million dollars.*

1784. — The second bank chartered in the country was the Massachusetts Bank of Boston, in the year 1784; and now, after the expiration of eighty-two years, it still exists and ranks among the soundest institutions of our country. Its first president was James Bowdoin; and, since its formation to the present time, it has had but nine presidents and nine cashiers. †

From that time to this, there has been a steady increase in the number of banks in the State, as well as in the whole country; and, as a natural consequence, there has been a corresponding increase in our paper-currency. We now have, in the State of Massachusetts alone, over two hundred banks, representing nearly eighty millions of capital, all but one of which are authorized by the General Government. The total number of national banks in the United States, March 17, 1866, was sixteen hundred and forty-three, with a capital of $412,693,236, and a circulation of $260,824,903. To this large amount of paper-money in circulation may be added about five hundred millions more, issued by the United States

---

* Appendix M.

† The Report of the Bank Commissioners of Massachusetts, for 1865, gives an interesting account of the system of banking adopted by that State; also some notice of the early paper-currency.

and by the several State banks, making the sum of nearly seven hundred and sixty millions of dollars of paper-money now in circulation in the United States.

Again war has thrown its dark shadow over our country, and again the Government have been obliged to resort to the expedient of our forefathers in issuing large amounts of paper-money, so that at this time the epithet of the paper-money country may be fittingly applied to the United States. This large issue of a paper-currency produces many of the same effects as in earlier years; prices of all commodities increase rapidly; the bills depreciate in value; and the spirit of speculation seems to have taken possession of our people. This depreciation of the currency, although very great at times during the past four years, has not been the occasion of so much general anxiety and depression as in the days of the Revolution; for the majority of our citizens have had full confidence in the strength of the Government, and in the ultimate redemption of its bills. In these remarks, it is of course understood, that we do not refer to the paper-currency of the South during the late rebellion; for, as is well known, their paper-money has become like so much waste paper, valuable only as material for the paper-mill.

Finally, let us bear in mind the importance of preserving all matter that may serve to illustrate in any way the finances of our times; so that the future antiquary will find abundant material to aid him in explaining to his day and generation the true condition of this epoch, as shown in the history of our currency and finances. It is the special province of this Society to care for and preserve the written history of to-day: let us not be backward in our duty, but lend a willing heart and a helping hand to add our mite to the fulfilment of so commendable an object.

APPENDIX.

A.

Roger Williams in his account of wampum, says of its use among the New-England Indians: "Their own is of two forts, one white, which they make of the ſtem or ſtock of the periwinkle, when all the ſhell is broken off; and of this fort, ſix of their ſmall beads, which they make with holes to ſtring their bracelets, are current with the Engliſh for a penny. The ſecond is black, inclining to blue, which is made of the ſhell of a fiſh, which ſome Engliſh call hens — poquahock; and of this fort, three make an Engliſh penny. One fathom of this their ſtringed money is worth five ſhillings."

B.

The first issue of paper money is probably rightfully attributed to the Chinese. Doolittle, in his "Social Life of the Chinese," says it was used by them in the ninth, and down to the fifteenth, century, when the issue of it was stopped: at the present time, however, it is again in use in China.

What was called card-money was adopted by the French in Canada, in 1687, redeemable in bills on France. This was at the time of an expedition by the French to subdue the Senecas. Probably this issue was not known of, by the English colonists of Massachusetts Bay, at the time they made their first issue of paper money, in 1690.

C.

The signers of the Bill of Credit, issued in 1690, as given on the bill exhibited at the meeting of the Historical Society, were John

Phillips, Adam Winthrop, and Penn Townsend. On the bill described by Mr. Drake, the signers were Elisha Hutchinson, John Walley, and Tim. Thornton.

Colonel John Phillips, of Charlestown, was Judge of Admiralty, Treasurer of the Province, and Representative from 1683 to 1686. In 1689, he was one of the Council of Safety; and, in 1691, one of the first Council under the new charter, which office he held until 1716. He was wounded in a fight with the Indians, at Casco Bay, in 1697. He died March, 1725, aged ninety-four.

Adam Winthrop, of Boston, was a man of prominence in the Massachusetts Colony, and was undoubtedly a grandson of Governor Winthrop. He was born in 1647, and graduated at Harvard College in 1668, a Representative in 1689–92, and, being a member of Mather's church, was named by the king, by advice of Mather, one of the Governor's Council under the new charter; which office he held from 1692 to his death. He was known as Hon. Adam Winthrop in his day, and was grandfather of Professor John Winthrop, the eminent Professor of Mathematics and Natural Philosophy in Harvard College from 1738 to 1779. He died in August, 1700.*

Penn Townsend was also a man of note in Boston, and held many prominent offices; was Speaker, Judge of the Court of Common Pleas, and was also a colonel of the militia. He died in 1727, aged seventy-five.

Elisha Hutchinson, of Boston, was grandfather of Governor Thomas Hutchinson. He was a Representative in 1680-3, and a councillor or assistant magistrate from 1684 till his death. In 1707, he was a colonel in the Port-Royal Expedition. He was also one of the first Council under the charter of William and Mary, in 1692. He died Dec. 10, 1717, aged seventy-seven.

John Walley was a Judge of the Superior Court of Massachusetts, and a member of the Council. He died in 1712, aged sixty-eight. In 1690, the year these bills were issued, he accompanied the expedition against Canada, being in command of the land-forces. The failure of this expedition caused the issuing of the bills of credit, which he afterwards, as a member of the General Court, was called upon to sign. His "Journal of the Campaign

---

* The information in relation to Adam Winthrop is obtained from his descendant, Hon. R. C. Winthrop.

in Canada" may be found in Hutchinson's "History of Massachusetts."

Timothy Thornton was a merchant of Boston, a Representative to the General Court in 1690, '93, '94, selectman of Boston in 1693, and one of the assessors in 1694. He appears to have been a man of some note in the town of Boston; but we have not been able to find any connected notice of him. We are indebted to Drake's "History of Boston" for many facts in regard to the signers of these bills. In Lossing's "Pictorial Field-Book of the Revolution" is a fac-simile of one of the bills of 1690, which has the same date and the same signers as that described by Drake. From the appearance of this fac-simile, we should judge it to have been taken from an engraved bill; as the seal, as well as other parts of the bill, seem to have been more carefully finished than in the written bill described in this Report.

D.

In 1692, an Act was passed by the "Great and General Court or Assembly of their Majesties' Province of the Massachusetts Bay," entitled "An Act, For Making the Former Bills of Credit to Pafs Current, in Future Payments, &c."

"Whereas, Their Majefties Affairs within this Province do require a fpeedy advance for the Defence of the Province, and the profecution of the War, againft their French and Indian enemies, and there being no Stock at prefent in the Treafury to fupply the fame or to defray other the neceffary charges for fupport of the Government, Be it therefore ordained and enacted that all Bills of Publick Creditt iffued forth by order of the Generall Court of the late Colony of Maffachufetts Bay, fhall pafs current within this Province in all payments equivalent to money, and in all publick payments at 5 per cent. advance. And for encouragement to fuch perfons as are poffeffors of faid Bills, to lend them for the fervice of the publick, it is further enacted that they fhall be fecured by the publick Taxes and other Revenues, and fhall be reimburft in money within twelve months."

E.

May 27, 1702, an "Act for Making and Emitting of Bills of Publick Credit," was passed, as follows: "Forafmuch as by reafon of the extream Scarcity of Money, and the want of other medium of Commerce, the Trade of this Province is greatly obftructed, and the affairs of the Government very much hindered; The payment of the Publick Debts and Taxes Retarded, and in great meafure rendered Impracticable, to the Difcouragement of Souldiers and Seamen necefilarily Employed in her Majefty's Service, in the defenfe of Her Majeftys Subjects and Interefts with the Province in this time of War."

For remedy whereof, it was enacted, "That there be forthwith imprinted a certain number of bills of credit on this Province in fuitable Sums from Two Shillings to Five Pounds which in the whole fhall amount to the Sum of Ten Thoufand Pounds & no more; which bills fhall be Indented and Stamped with fuch ftamps as the Governour and Council fhall project and direct; And be Signed by a Committee to be Nominated and Appointed by this Court, they or any three of them; and of the Tenor following, That is to fay

No. ( )   S
                  20

"This Indented Bill of Twenty Shillings due from the Province of Maffachufetts-Bay in New-England, to the Poffeffor thereof, fhall be in value equal to Money: And fhall be accordingly accepted by the Treafurer and Receivers Subordinate to him, in all Publick Payments, and for any Stock at any time in the Treafury. Bofton November the Twenty Firft, Anno 1702. By order of the Great and General Court or Affembly.

                          "J. R.
                          "E. H. } *Committee*."*
                          "N. B

F.

The bill of 1713 reads as follows:—

No.   EIGHTEEN PENCE.   (2419)

This Bill of one Shilling and Sixpence Indented, due from the

---

* From Massachusetts Colonial Laws.

Province of the Maſſachuſetts Bay in New England to yᵉ Poſſeſ-
for thereof ſhall be in value equal to money: And ſhall be accordingly accepted by the Treaſurer and Receivers ſubordinate to
him in all Publick payments: and for any Stock at any time in
the Treaſury, Boſton October the fourteenth 1713 By Order of
the Great and General Court or Aſſembly.

[Seal.]   A WINTHROP
          A DAVENPORT
          Wᵐ PAYNE
          SAMˡ CHECKLEY   } Comᵗᵗᵉᵉ

1714
1718
1719
1721
1722
1723
1725
1727
1731

G.

The Land Bank Company of 1714, in their project for starting
the Company, proposed to give, out of their net profits, to several
charitable objects: " Four Hundred Pounds per Annum to the Uſe
of an Hoſpital or Charity School, for the Support and Education of
the poor Children in the Town of Boſton, &c. — — Provided the
Inhabitants and Freeholders of the Town of Boſton, do, at or
before their General Meeting in March, One Thouſand Seven
Hundred and Fifteen, order the Treaſurer to accept the ſaid Bank
Bills in payment of Town Taxes and Aſſeſſment." Also, " Two
Hundred Pounds per Annum to be paid to the Treaſurer of Harvard College in Cambridge, for the Uſes following, Viz. Twenty
Pounds per Annum for a Mathematical Proffeſſor Reſiding there
&c. — — — Forty Pounds per Annum for the Encouragement
of three Graduates Reſiding there, until they take their Maſters
Degree, &c, — — — One Hundred Pounds per Annum for the
ſupport of ſix Miniſters Sons to be equally divided among them &c.
— — Forty Pounds per Annum to a Proffeſſor of Phyſick and
Anatomy, Reſiding there provided he Read a Lecture once a
month, on that ſubject." Provision was also made to give
" Twenty Pounds per Annum towards the further Support of a
Publick Grammar School in each County, &c &c."*

These various benevolent propoſitions were undoubtedly made
to induce the public to be more willing to subscribe to the project,

---

* " A Projection For Erecting a Bank of Credit in Boston, New England, Founded
on Land Security. 1714."

rather than from any particular design to assist these educational enterprises: that this was the opinion of many at the time, the pamphlets published in objection to the project testify.

H.

The Trustees appointed under the act of May, 1714, were Andrew Belcher, one of the Council, and a Representative (he died in 1717); Addington Davenport, Clerk of the Court, and Judge of the Supreme Court; Thomas Hutchinson, a member of the Council, father of Governor Thomas Hutchinson; John White, a prominent citizen of Boston; and Edward Hutchinson, brother of Thomas, a Judge of Probate, &c.

I.

From the Massachusetts General Court Records, of 1737, we take the following act authorizing the issuing of small bills:—

"An Act for making Two Thoufand fix Hundred and twenty-five Pounds in fmall Bills of feveral Denominations to be Exchanged for larger Bills by the Province Treafurer.

PREAMBLE. —*Whereas*, great Inconveniences and Difficulties have arifen to the Affairs and Trade of this Province for
want of fmall money or change;

𝔅𝔢 𝔦𝔱 𝔈𝔫𝔞𝔠𝔱𝔢𝔡 𝔟𝔶 𝔓𝔦𝔰 𝔈𝔵𝔠𝔢𝔩𝔩𝔢𝔫𝔠𝔶 𝔱𝔥𝔢 𝔊𝔬𝔟𝔢𝔯𝔫𝔬𝔲𝔯, 𝔆𝔬𝔲𝔫𝔠𝔦𝔩 𝔞𝔫𝔡 𝔕𝔢𝔭𝔯𝔢𝔰𝔢𝔫𝔱𝔞𝔱𝔦𝔟𝔢𝔰 𝔦𝔫 𝔊𝔢𝔫𝔢𝔯𝔞𝔩 𝔆𝔬𝔲𝔯𝔱 𝔞𝔰𝔰𝔢𝔪𝔟𝔩𝔢𝔡, 𝔞𝔫𝔡 𝔱𝔥𝔢 𝔄𝔲𝔱𝔥𝔬𝔯𝔦𝔱𝔶 𝔬𝔣 𝔱𝔥𝔢 𝔰𝔞𝔪𝔢,

That the Committee already appointed by this Court for the making of Bills of Credit of the new Tenor, be and hereby are directed to take effectual care, that there be forthwith made and imprinted on good paper, to the Amount of Two Thousand six Hundred and twenty-five Pounds in Pennys, Two Pences, Three Pences, Four Pences, Five Pences and Six Pences, of Each Denomination Thirty Thoufand Bills of the following Figures and Inscriptions."

Here follows an engraving, showing the different denominations and forms of each.

"Which Bills, when ready, faid Committee are to deliver to the Treafurer of the Province, by him to be exchanged for other Bills of the Province to such Persons as come for the same, but not less than Twenty Shillings at one time; and that the said Bills shall pass in all Payments as other the Bills of this Province of the New Tenor do according to Law, and that the Bills received by the Treasurer in Lieu of the aforesaid small Bills, shall be burnt to Ashes, by a Committee of this Court appointed for that purpose."

There was also a provision, in the enactment, against counterfeiting or forging these bills.

J.

In August, 1758, the following notice by the Sheriff of Suffolk County was printed in the "Boston News Letter:"—

"To be sold at public Auction, at the Exchange Tavern in Boston, To morrow at noon. The Dwelling House, Malt-House, and other buildings, with the Garden and land adjoining, and the Wharf, Dock and Flats, before the same, being part of the Estate of the late *Samuel Adams*, Esq., deceased, and is scituate near Bull-Wharf, at the lower end of Summer Street, in Boston aforesaid, the said Estate being taken by Warrant or execution under the hand and seal of the Hon. Commissioners for the more speedy finishing the Land Bank or Manufactory Scheme. The Plan of the ground and the terms of payment may be known by enquiring of

"STEPHEN GREENLEAF."

In answer to this advertisement, there appeared the following letter in the "News Letter" of Aug. 16, which shows the extent of Mr. Adams's threats:—

"TO STEPHEN GREENLEAF, ESQ.

"SIR,

"I observe your Advertisement for the sale of the Estate of *Samuel Adams*, Esq., Director of the Land Bank Company. Your predecessor Col. Pollard had the same affair in hand five years before his death; but with all his known firmness of mind, he never brought the matter to any conclusion; and *his Precept*, I am told, is not returned to this Day.—The reason was—he, as well as myself, was advised by gentlemen of the law, that his proceeding was illegal and unwarrantable; and therefore he very prudently declined entering so far into this affair as to subject his own Estate

Specimen of a Manufactory Bank Bill of 1741. Photographed from an original bill in possession of American Antiquarian Society.

to danger. How far your determination may lead you, you know better than I. I would only beg leave, with freedom to affure you, that I am advifed and determined to profecute to the law any perfon whomfoever who fhall trefpafs upon that Eftate; and remain

"Your humble servant

"SAMUEL ADAMS.

"BOSTON Aug. 16 1758."

That this letter probably had some weight with the sheriff would appear from the fact that the sale was adjourned from time to time. In the "News Letter" of September, 1758, we find the following notice in regard to the sale:—

"The fale of Mr. *Adams'* Eftate, which was adjourned to Friday, the 22d of September, is further adjourned, to Friday, the 29th inst: Attendance will be given THAT DAY at the Royal Exchange Tavern, from XII to I o'clock by

"S GREENLEAF."

It is probable that the subscription to aid Mr. Adams in paying the claim caused the final postponement of the sale.

K.

In the collection of the Antiquarian Society is a specimen of a Manufactory Company bill, dated in 1741, but without signers. This bill was undoubtedly engraved in England, as it is much finer than any engraved in this country at that period. That this bill was probably issued by some company similar to the Land Bank Company there can be but little doubt; but, after inquiry of several who were supposed to be conversant with the history of Essex County, where this bill seems to have originated, we have been able to learn nothing definite in regard to it. It reads as follows:—

THE BANK BILL. Two SHILLINGS. We jointly and feverally, for our felves and partners, promife to take this Bill as Two Shillings, lawful Silver Money, at Six Shillings, and Eight Pence p^r Ounce, in all Payments Trade and Bufiness, & for Stock in our Treafury at any Time, & to pay the fame at that Eftimate on Demand, to Mr James Eveleth or Order, in the Produce or Manufactures enumerated 'in our scheme; as recorded in the County of Essex's Records, for Value rec^d Dated at Ipfwich, the Firft Day of May, 1741

L.

The Massachusetts Bills of Credit issued in 1775, and known as the "sword-in-hand" money, read as follows:—

Colony of the Maffachufetts Bay } Decm.r 7. 1775.

The Poffeffor of this Bill fhall be paid, by the Treafurer of this Colony Three Shillings & four-pence Lawfull money, by the 7 Day of Decm.r 1781, which Bill fhall be received for the aforefaid fum in all payments at the Treasury, and in all other payments by order of the General Assembly

[Seal.]   Committee { J WHEELER.

The Massachusetts revolutionary issue, under authority of the Continental Congress, was in the following form:—

STATE OF MASSACHUSETTS

No. 14,277   One Dollar

ONE DOLLAR

The Poffeffor of this Bill fhall be paid one Spanifhed milled Dollar by the Thirty-firft Day of December, One Thoufand Seven Hundred and Eighty-Six, with Intereft, at the rate of Five per Centum per Annum, by the State of Maffachufetts Bay, according to an Act of the Legiflature of the faid State, of the Fifth Day of May, 1780.

Tho? DAWES
R CRANCH

Interest.	s.	d.	q.
Annually ..	0	3	2¼
Monthly ...	0	0	1¼

On the reverse,—

United States
ONE DOLLAR.

Seal with motto, *Depressa Resurget*.
Printed by HALL and SELLERS

The United States enfure the Payment of the within Bill, and will draw Bills of Exchange for the Intereft annually, if demanded, according to a Refolution of CONGRESS, of the 18th of March, 1780

Peter Boyer

The United States.

The first emission of paper money by the Continental Congress was in June, 1775: at that time it was enacted, "That a fum not exceeding two millions of Spanifh milled dollars be emitted by the Congrefs in bills of credit for the defence of America." New emissions were from time to time authorized by Congress, until, in 1780, the sum of two hundred millions of dollars had been issued, none of which had been redeemed.

The large amount of paper money in circulation caused a great depreciation in its value ; and it is said, that, in 1780, it took seven hundred dollars to buy a pair of shoes: a handkerchief cost one hundred dollars, and a skein of silk ten dollars.

The following table, showing the depreciation of the Continental money, is taken from "The Historical Magazine," vol. iv. : * —

"*Value of* $1000 *Continental Dollars in Specie on the First Day of every month, agreeable to late Resolutions of Congress.*"

DATE.	Continental Bills.	Value in Hard Dollars.	DATE.	Continental Bills.	Value in Hard Dollars.
1777. September	$1,000	$1,000	1779. January	$1,000	$134
1777. October	1,000	911	1779. February	1,000	115
1777. November	1,000	828	1779. March	1,000	110
1777. December	1,000	754	1779. April	1,000	90
1778. January	1,000	685	1779. May	1,000	82
1778. February	1,000	623	1779. June	1,000	74
1778. March	1,000	571	1779. July	1,000	67
1778. April	1,000	497	1779. August	1,000	61
1778. May	1,000	434	1779. September	1,000	55
1778. June	1,000	378	1779. October	1,000	49
1778. July	1,000	330	1779. November	1,000	43
1778. August	1,000	287	1779. December	1,000	38
1778. September	1,000	250	1780. January	1,000	34
1778. October	1,000	215	1780. February	1,000	30
1778. November	1,000	183	1780. March	1,000	26
1778. December	1,000	157	1780. April	1,000	25

In February, 1781, $7,500 of Continental money was worth but $100 in specie; and, during the year, it became worthless.

M.

J. J. DIXWELL, Esq., President of the Massachussetts Bank, has kindly furnished a list of the Presidents and Cashiers of that bank from its organization to the present time.

PRESIDENTS.

James Bowdoin	Chosen March 22, 1784.
William Phillips	January 5, 1786.
Jonathan Mason	January 2, 1797.
Samuel Eliot	June 18, 1798.
William Phillips, Jr.	January 5, 1804.
William Parsons	June 25, 1827.
Jonathan Phillips	October 31, 1836.
William Parsons, Jr.	May 27, 1840.
John L. Gardner, *pro tem.*	January 22, 1847.
John J. Dixwell	February 25, 1847.

* In quoting this table, the value expressed in tenths of a dollar is omitted.

CASHIERS.

Samuel Osgood	Chosen May 20, 1784.
Peter Roe Dalton	January 31, 1785.
John Lowell	March 15, 1792.
James Thwing	June 10, 1793.
Joseph Head	November 24, 1814.
Charles P. Phelps	January 3, 1816.
Samuel Payson	September 29, 1817.
James Dodd	November 24, 1836.
Henry K. Frothingham	May 28, 1863.

James Dodd was connected with the bank, in various capacities, fifty-four years consecutively.

List of Books and Pamphlets, in the Library of the American Antiquarian Society, at Worcester, which refer to the Colonial or Continental Paper-Currency of the United States.

Objections to the Bank of Credit Lately projected at Boston, Being a Letter upon that Occasion to John Burril Esq; Speaker to the House of Representatives for the Province of Massachusetts Bay in New England. Boston:	1714
Letter from one in Boston to his Friend in the Country, In answer to a Letter directed to John Burril Esq Speaker to the House of Representatives, for the Province of Massachusetts Bay in New England. Boston:	1714
A Vindication of the Bank of Credit, Projected in Boston from the Aspersions of Paul Dudley Esq in a Letter directed by him to John Burril Esq, Late Speaker &c Boston:	1714
A Vindication of the Remarks of One in the Country upon the distressed State of Boston, from some Exceptions made against 'Em in a Letter to Mr Colman	1720
A Project for the Emission of an Hundred Thousand Pounds of Province Bills, in such a manner as to keep their credit up Equal to Silver, and to bring an Hundred Thousand Pounds of Silver Money into the Country in a few years Boston:	1720
Some Proposals to benefit the Province Boston:	1720
A word of Comfort to a Melancholy Country, or the Bank of Credit erected in Massachusetts Bay, Fairly Defended by a Discovery of the Great Benefit, accruing by it to the Whole Province &c, Boston:	1721
The Melancholy State of the Province considered in a Letter From a Gentleman in Boston, to his Friend in the Country Boston:	1736
A Letter to a Member of the Honorable House of Representatives on the Present State of the Bills of Credit. Boston:	1736

Observations on the Scheme for 60,000l in Bills of a New Tenour
Boston: 1738
A Discourse concerning the currencies of the British Plantations in America, Especially with regard to their Paper money, more particularly in relation to the Province of the Massachusetts Bay in New England Boston: 1740
Postcript to a Discourse concerning the Currencies of the British Plantations in America. 1740
An Inquiry into the Nature and Uses of Money more especially of the bills of Publick Credit, Old Tenor &c Boston: 1740
A Letter Relating to a Medium of Trade in the Province of the Massachusetts Bay Printed at the New Printing Office, opposite to the South East Corner of the Town House Boston: 1740
A Letter to ——— Merchant in London, concerning a late Combination in the Province of Mass.-Bay. in N.E.,— to impose or force a Private Currency called Land Bank Money. Printed for the Publick Good 1741
A Letter to the Merchant in London to whom is directed a Printed Letter relating to the Manufactory Undertaking, dated New England Boston Feb'y 21 1741 Printed for the Publick Good.
A Letter from a Country Gentleman at Boston to his Friends in the Country Boston: 1740
A Brief Account of the Rise, Progress and Present State of the Paper Currency of New England &c Boston: 1749
An Essay concerning Silver and Paper Currency more especially with regard to the British Colonies in New England Boston: N. D.
Consideration on Lowering the Value of Gold coins within the Province of the Massachusetts-Bay Boston: 1761
Observations on the Nature and use of Paper Credit and the peculiar advantages to be derived from it, in North America &c Phila: 1781
Considerations on the Bank of North America, Phila: 1785
Letter addressed to the Legislators of the several States, composing the Federal Union recommending an uniform Continental Currency. &c, New York: 1796
Path to Riches. An Inquiry into the Origin and Use of Money, and into the Principles of Stocks and Banks, To which are subjoined some Thoughts respecting a Bank for the Commonwealth. James Sullivan Boston: 1792
An Historical Account of Massachusetts Currency. J. B. Felt.
Boston: 1839
Historical Sketch of Continental-Paper Money. S. Breck. Phila.: N. D.
Notes on Ante-Revolutionary Currency and Politics, communicated to the New-England Historical and Genealogical Register. By A. H. Ward. July, 1860
An Historical Sketch of the Paper-Money issued by Pennsylvania. H. Phillips, Jr. Phila.: 1862
A History of the Bills of Credit or Paper-Money issued by New York, from 1709 to 1789. J. H. Hickcox. Albany: 1866

Historical Account of Connecticut-Currency, Continental-Money, and the Finances of the Revolution. By Henry Bronson. (Published in vol. i., papers of the New-Haven Colony Historical Society.) 1865
Historical Sketches of American Paper-Currency. 2 vols. II. Phillips, Jr. Roxbury: 1866

Paper-Money in the Collection of the American Antiquarian Society.

The whole number of bills, issued previous to 1789, in the collection is 286; of which 47 were issued before 1775; viz., by Massachusetts, 7; by New Hampshire, 1; Rhode Island, 3; Maryland, 17; Virginia, 1; Pennsylvania, 16; Georgia, 2.

Of those issued by the States from 1775 to 1789, there are 155 specimens, divided as follows: Massachusetts, 58; Vermont, 3; Connecticut, 26; New-Hampshire, 5; Rhode Island, 19; Pennsylvania, 15; Delaware, 2; Virginia, 12; New York, 5; New Jersey, 4; Maryland, 5; Georgia, 1.

Of those issued by the Continental Congress, there are eighty-four specimens, mostly in good order.

REMARKS

ON THE

EARLY PAPER CURRENCY

OF

MASSACHUSETTS:

Read before the American Antiquarian Society,

April 25, 1866,

BY NATHANIEL PAINE.

www.ingramcontent.com/pod-product-compliance
Lightning Source LLC
Chambersburg PA
CBHW021949160426
43195CB00011B/1291